CHINESE
AND JAPANESE
CRAFTS
And Their Cultural
Backgrounds

Also by Jeremy Comins

ART FROM FOUND OBJECTS

ESKIMO CRAFTS
and their Cultural Backgrounds

LATIN AMERICAN CRAFTS
and their Cultural Backgrounds

SLOTTED SCULPTURE FROM CARDBOARD

TOTEMS, DECOYS, AND COVERED WAGONS:
Cardboard Constructions from Early American Life

CHINESE AND JAPANESE CRAFTS
And Their Cultural Backgrounds

JEREMY COMINS

Lothrop, Lee & Shepard Company

A Division of William Morrow & Company   •   New York

To Eleanor

Drawings and photographs by the author
except where noted.

Library of Congress Cataloging in Publication Data
Comins, Jeremy.
Chinese and Japanese crafts and their cultural backgrounds.

SUMMARY: Instructions for making netsuke,
lacquer ware, puppets, masks, and other objects
in the style of traditional Chinese and Japanese crafts,
with notes on their cultural background.
1. Handicraft—China—Juvenile literature.
2. Handicraft—Japan—Juvenile literature.
[1. Handicraft—China.   2. Handicraft—Japan]
I. Title.   TT101.C65   745.5   77-28835
ISBN 0-688-41844-9   ISBN 0-688-51844-3 lib. bdg.

First Edition

1   2   3   4   5   6   7   8   9   10

Acknowledgments

I wish to express my thanks to Harry and Edith Comins for their encouragement in my work, and to Eleanor Comins for her help in discussing the projects.

Mr. Raymond S. T. Leung of the Chinese Information Service was most helpful in supplying much of the background material.

Contents

ABOVE: The Great Wall of China as photographed on a NASA flight, September 3, 1976. *National Aeronautics and Space Administration; reproduction courtesy of Eros Data Center*

BELOW: The Great Wall of China as represented in a Chinese cut paper design. *Chinese Cut Paper Designs, Dover Publications, Inc.*

Introduction

For centuries, China and Japan have produced works of art and craft that to this day remain unsurpassed in their beauty and craftsmanship. A fine lacquer vase, hundreds of years old, will blend with the most modern of home decor, so classic is its design and so perfect its execution.

Oriental accomplishments range from tiny ivory carvings (netsuke) from Japan, no longer than an inch and a half and perfect in every detail, to the massive Great Wall of China, winding for 1,500 miles over mountain and plain, which was constructed in the third century B.C. as a defense against invasions from the North.

It would be impossible to cover here all of the crafts of these two great cultures. Some of them, calligraphy and pottery, for example, require techniques or equipment beyond the scope of this book. Others such as origami, the Japanese art of paper-folding, have been widely covered elsewhere.

I have selected crafts of China and Japan that can be adapted to simple construction in easily obtained materials and still exemplify the style and spirit of Oriental art. By making these projects you will get the satisfaction that comes from having created something that is individually your own; at the same time, I believe you will gain an appreciation of the unique and different approach of the Far Eastern artist.

Ivory netsuke, ¾ inch high and 1 9/16 inches long, representing the 12 signs of the zodiac. Contemporary Japanese. *Courtesy Donald H. Silberberg*

Dragon stenciled onto a sweater. A small stone is set in for the eye.

A NOTE ON DRAGONS
AND THE COLOR RED

Although many motifs appear in Chinese and Japanese art, the dragon and the color red have particular significance. In the West, the dragon is a symbol of Evil. In the European legend, St. George fights the fearsome dragon to save the fair maiden. In China, however, the dragon symbolizes all things good: Wisdom, Justice, Dignity, Benevolence, and Good Luck. In the East it would indeed be St. George's ally.

The color red also represents all things that are good. Thus it is commonly used in the art and craft of China.

11

HOW TO USE THIS BOOK

Each chapter gives step-by-step instructions for making an object inspired by a traditional Chinese or Japanese one. In addition, design source material and photographs of the work of master Oriental artists are included to help you branch out and create your own variations on these projects. Information about where to obtain the tools and supplies used, as well as a glossary and suggestions for further reading, appears at the end of the book.

Miniature Sculpture and Netsuke

Carvings of bone and ivory have been discovered in China dating back to the Shang Dynasty (c. 1523–c. 1028 B.C.). Surviving ancient paintings and manuscripts indicate these small sculpted decorations were worn by dignitaries as part of their ceremonial dress. With the establishment of the T'ang Dynasty in the seventh century A.D. the use of ivory became more extensive in China, and it has continued in popularity as an art medium up to the present.

In Japan toward the eighteenth century it became fashionable to wear seal boxes (inro) and other kinds of pouches around the waist, since the clothing of the time had no pockets. A small toggle called a netsuke served to hold the hanging pouch or seal box in place on a cord. Although mainly functional, the netsuke soon became a highly decorative object, intricately carved in animal, human, plant, insect, or other motifs. Two holes were drilled in the back so a cord could pass through the form.

The netsuke was carved from wood, ivory, or other materials, and to be suitable for wearing it had to be small, about one and a half to three inches long, rounded and smooth to fit comfortably in the hands of the owner. Many techniques of larger sculpture were applied to the carving of netsuke.

LEFT: Ivory netsuke, rat, 1⅜ inches high and 1⅞ inches long.
The eyes are of ebony.
Japanese, 19th century.
Courtesy Donald H. Silberberg

RIGHT: Ivory netsuke, woodpile,
1¾ inches high and
1¼ inches wide.
Contemporary Japanese.
Courtesy Donald H. Silberberg

14

Ivory netsuke, an immortal, 4¼ inches high. Japanese, 18th century.
Courtesy of The Brooklyn Museum

ABOVE: Ivory netsuke, squirrel, 1½ inches high and 1¾ inches long. Contemporary Japanese. *Courtesy Donald H. Silberberg*

BELOW: Jade girdle-pendant, horse, 1⅞ inches by 2⅝ inches. Chinese, Han Dynasty. *The Metropolitan Museum of Art, Gift of Samuel T. Peters*

Jade girdle-pendant, man, $2\frac{5}{8}$ inches by $1\frac{5}{16}$ inches. Chinese, Han Dynasty. *The Metropolitan Museum of Art, Gift of Samuel T. Peters*

With the introduction in Japan of Western dress, netsuke are no longer in common use. But they are now sought by collectors as examples of fine miniature sculpture, and modern Japanese artists are carving them to meet collectors' demands.

17

TOP: Ivory netsuke, frog, 1 1/16th inches high. Japanese, 18th century. *Courtesy of The Brooklyn Museum*

BOTTOM: Ivory netsuke, sage and demon, 1 3/8 inches high. Japanese, 18th century. *Courtesy of The Brooklyn Museum*

In view of the fact that it took master artists and crafts-people to produce these miniature sculptures, it would be unreasonable to expect the average person to be able to carve one. We can, however, by combining a small amount of carving with painted details, capture some of the charm of these masterpieces in miniature.

18

HAPPY MAN NETSUKE

Our first netsuke depicts a happy Oriental man. We will make ours about the same size as the original, which was also carved from wood.

Materials
2 pieces of balsa wood 1½ x 3 x ¼-inch
1 piece of balsa wood 1 x 1 x ¼-inch
1 sheet tracing paper
X-acto knife (#1 if possible)
pencil and eraser

emery boards and fine sandpaper
Elmer's glue
light yellow ochre acrylic paint
burnt umber acrylic paint
(Acrylic paint is soluble in water and dries waterproof. It
is sold in tubes in art, hobby, and some toy stores.)
fine-pointed watercolor brush (#2 if possible)
2 paper cups for mixing paint

How to Make It
1. Figure 1 shows the outline of the basic parts of the
sculpture, full-scale.
2. Trace the three sections required to make the sculpture
from Figures 2, 3, and 4.
3. Cut out these paper sections and outline them lightly
in pencil on the balsa sheets.

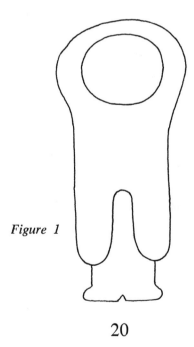

Figure 1

20

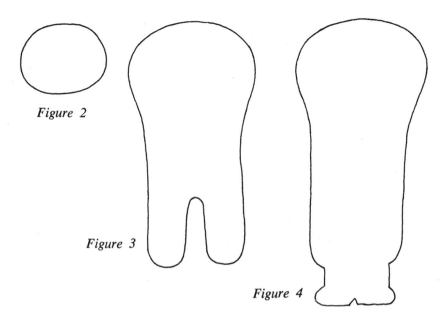

Figure 2

Figure 3

Figure 4

4. With your X-acto knife, cut out the balsa sections and then smooth the outlines of the pieces with the emery board. Glue together as shown in Figure 5.

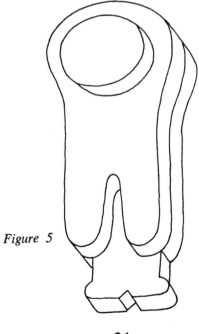

Figure 5

21

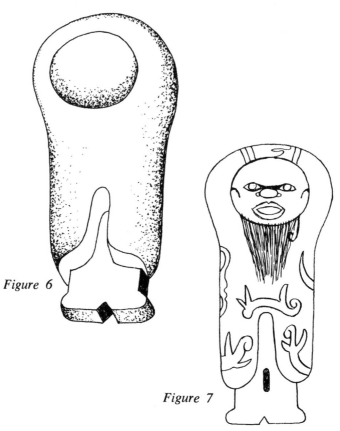

Figure 6

Figure 7

5. Round off the edges of the sculpture with the emery board as shown in Figure 6. Use the rough side of the emery board first, then the smooth side.

6. Dilute the light yellow ochre acrylic paint with water in a paper cup, so that it is thin enough to apply smoothly without streaking. Paint the sculpture with three coats of paint, sanding lightly with fine sandpaper between coats.

7. Sketch the details (Figure 7) in pencil and carefully paint them with a diluted mixture of burnt umber. Use only the tip of the brush.

Your sculpture is now finished.

SITTING HORSE NETSUKE

The second netsuke is derived from an ivory carving of a horse, and like the Happy Man ours will be made about the same size as the original.

Materials
2 pieces of balsa wood $1\frac{1}{2}$ x 3 x $\frac{1}{4}$-inch
1 piece of balsa wood 1 x 1 x $\frac{1}{4}$-inch
All other materials are the same as for the Happy Man.

How to Make It
The procedure is the same as outlined for the Happy Man. However, when tracing sections shown in Figures 9, 10, and 11, you will need to make two of Figure 10, one for each side of the animal.
Figure 12 shows a drawing of the completed sculpture to help in painting the details.

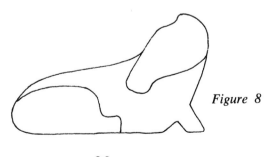

Figure 8

23

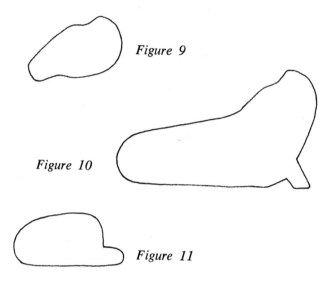

Figure 9

Figure 10

Figure 11

Figure 12

ASIATIC RAM NETSUKE

The third netsuke represents an Asiatic ram. The original was carved in wood by a Chinese artist.

Materials
2 pieces of balsa wood 1½ x 2½ x ¼-inch
1 piece of balsa wood 1 x 1¼ x ¼-inch
The other materials are the same as for the first two projects.

How to Make It
The procedure is the same as for the others. Figures 13 through 16 show the sections, and Figure 17 will aid in painting the details.

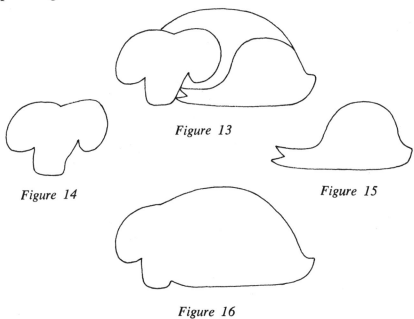

Figure 13

Figure 14

Figure 15

Figure 16

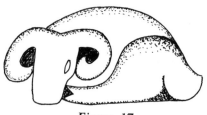

Figure 17

If you have a coping saw or small table-model jigsaw you might try making these sculptures from ¼-inch-thick pine, which is sold in lumberyards. Pine, being a harder wood than balsa, will be less susceptible to denting.

You might also try to adapt your own design from the photographs shown by following the techniques employed in the other netsuke projects. Determine the basic outlines of an object and how they can be represented in simple sections; then cut, smooth, glue, round off, and paint as you did above.

Kokeshi Dolls

Kokeshi, the traditional Japanese folk dolls, have been made in northeastern Japan since the early seventeenth century. Originally, the head and body were simple, lathe-turned wooden forms devoid of attached decoration. Details were painted on in graceful strokes, leaving much of the natural wood exposed. A clear lacquer finish was then applied to seal and protect the surface.

A well-designed kokeshi has the graceful simplicity of a sculpture, which for me holds a special appeal. Many modern kokeshi dolls show the use of fabric or wood additions to the basic form, and are coming to more closely

27

resemble conventional dolls: representational objects rather than abstract forms. But our kokeshi will attempt to capture the spirit of the earlier versions.

Traditional Japanese
kokeshi doll,
8 inches high.
*From the collection
of the author*

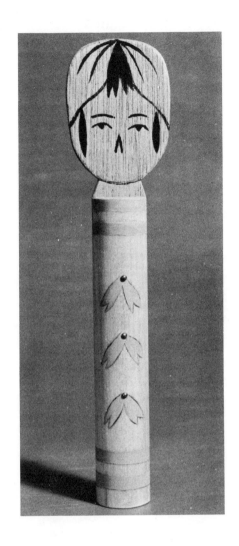

FIRST KOKESHI

Materials
wooden mop handle or broomstick (unpainted, if possible),
or a piece of wooden dowel about ¾-inch in diameter and
   6 inches long

heavy cardboard, non-corrugated
medium and fine sandpaper
saw
scissors
vise (optional)
Elmer's glue
light yellow ochre acrylic paint, and your choice of other
    colors
#2 watercolor brush
paper cup for mixing paint
roundheaded nails (optional)

How to Make It

1. With a saw, cut a 6-inch length from the mop handle for the body of the kokeshi. Place the wood in a vise, or hold it firmly on a table top with one hand while you saw with the other (Figure 1).

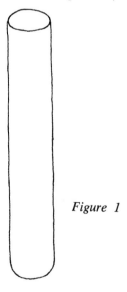

Figure 1

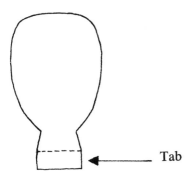

Tab

Figure 2

2. Draw the shape of the head on the cardboard. You can try different shapes, as long as the width of the tab is the same as the width of the body (Figure 2). Cut out the head with scissors.

3. Saw a slot about ½-inch deep across the top of the body (Figure 3).

4. Sand the body well. First use medium sandpaper, then fine.

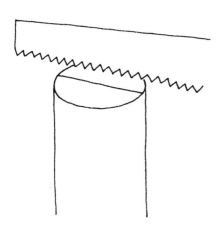

Figure 3

31

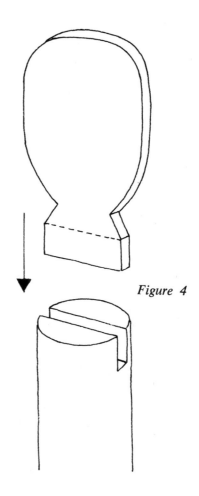

Figure 4

5. Glue the head into the slot cut in step 3 (Figure 4). Many traditional kokeshi dolls were left natural wood with just the features and designs applied in paint. If the body of your kokeshi is made from unpainted dowel, just paint the cardboard head with a light yellow ochre to give it a woodlike look. Dilute your paint with water in a paper cup. If your doll was made from a painted mop handle,

give the whole doll two coats of light yellow ochre. You can then paint the features in your own choice of colors (Figure 5).

6. Roundheaded nails can be hammered into the body as decorative accents (Figure 6).

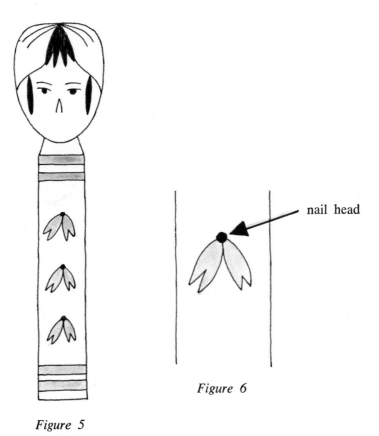

nail head

Figure 6

Figure 5

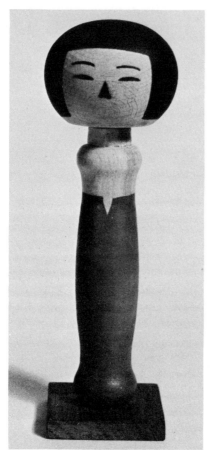 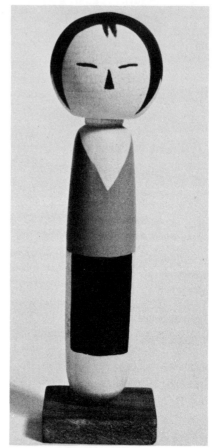

SECOND KOKESHI

You can create a more rounded doll by using a lathe-turned tool handle for the body and a wooden cabinet knob for the head. Many lumber and tool supply centers have bins of natural wood replacement tool handles (Figure 7) and cabinet knobs (Figure 8).

Some hobby stores will carry wooden beads ¾-inch to

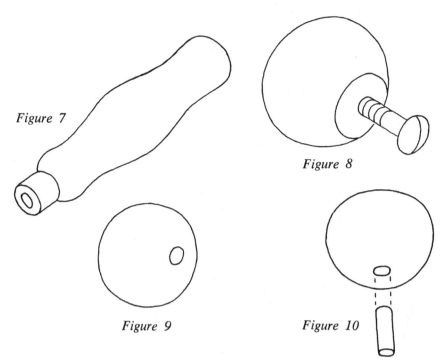

Figure 7

Figure 8

Figure 9

Figure 10

1 inch in diameter. Such a bead can also be used for the head of a small doll (Figure 9).

Materials
natural wood tool handle
a round natural wood knob or bead
dowel stick. Choose the size that will fit snugly into the
    hole in the knob or bead.
clear paste wax or lemon oil
The other materials are the same as indicated for the first kokeshi.

How to Make It
After you choose the components of your doll, cut a short length of dowel stick and glue it into the head (Figure 10).

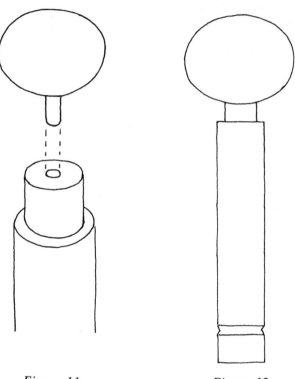

Figure 11   Figure 12

Then glue the head section into the handle (Figure 11). Figure 12 shows the completely assembled doll.

Sand well with fine sandpaper. Then apply the features and decorative details as indicated for the first kokeshi. You may modify the designs shown in the photographs as you wish.

When the paint is dry, apply a thin coat of wax or lemon oil over the surface of the doll. This will give a finished look to the natural wood and protect it from dirt or smudging.

If your kokeshi is too top heavy to stand upright, glue a small square of wood to the bottom as a base.

Festival and Theater Crafts

Festivals of all kinds play an important part in the Chinese and Japanese ways of life. They are held throughout the year to celebrate the seasons, commemorate special events, and to honor different members of the family, ancestors, or gods.

In both countries the most important is the New Year's Festival, a time for settling accounts, feasting on special foods, visiting, and exchanging cards and gifts. Firecrackers ward off evil spirits, and a variety of customs are observed to insure good luck and good fortune in the New Year.

New Year's Festival Dragon Dance in China. Notice the length of the dragon. *Chinese Information Service, New York*

In China, the New Year's celebration ends with the Feast of Lanterns, on the fifteenth day of the new moon. Originally, the lanterns were torches, lit to help the revelers seek and find the benevolent spirits. Today this festival is a community carnival, which includes a Dragon Dance. A large dragon with a papier-maché head and a cloth tail is manipulated by the dancers as they wind through the streets. The Cantonese, in southern China, also do a Lion Dance. The lion, shorter than the dragon, re-

38

ABOVE: New Year's Festival Lion Dance as performed on Mott Street, New York City, 1977. The shorter lion is better suited to narrow city streets.

BELOW: Closeup of the lion's head.

quires fewer dancers and thus is better suited than the dragon to the New Year's Festival as it is celebrated by Chinese-Americans on narrow Mott Street in New York City.

You can make a smaller version of the traditional dragon, which you can use at parties or other festival occasions. The one shown is designed to be handled by two people, but it can be made any length by increasing the number of tail sections and wooden sticks.

Adaptation of the traditional dragon to simple cardboard construction. The dragon can be made longer with additional paper sections and sticks.

NEW YEAR'S FESTIVAL DRAGON

Materials
2-foot x 15-inch piece of corrugated cardboard
1-foot x 5-foot piece of corrugated cardboard
You can get these pieces from a carton. Try to get cardboard without any printing on it.
Elmer's glue
ruler
large scissors
wrapping paper
2 strips of wood, approximately 24 x 1 x ⅜-inch
acrylic paint (red, white, black)
½-inch paintbrush; small #2 or round-pointed paintbrush
You can substitute large markers if you are working on unprinted cardboard.

How to Make It
1. Sketch the head and eye sections in pencil on the cardboard as shown in Figure 1.

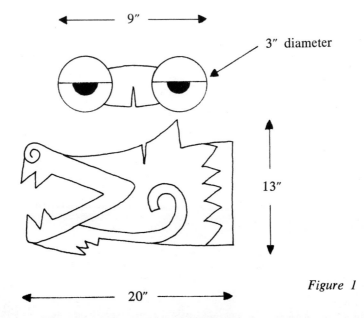

Figure 1

2. Cut them out with scissors.

3. Cut a tapered slot in the head and eye sections. The widest part of the slot should be as wide as the thickness of the cardboard. This will insure a tight fit (Figure 2).

4. Join the eye section to the head (Figure 3) and glue in place.

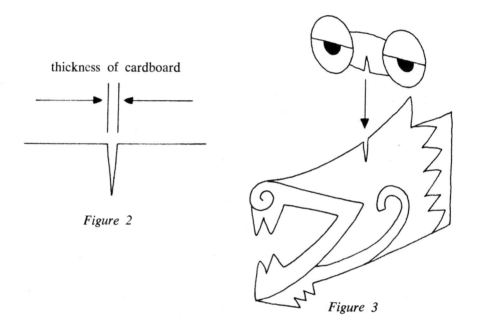

thickness of cardboard

Figure 2

Figure 3

5. The head can now be painted—two coats are best. Traditionally, the colors used are red, yellow, green, or black. Choose whichever color you wish and outline the details with one of the others. The eyes can be painted white.

6. The pictured dragon's tail was made from striped wrapping paper, which came in a package containing two sheets,

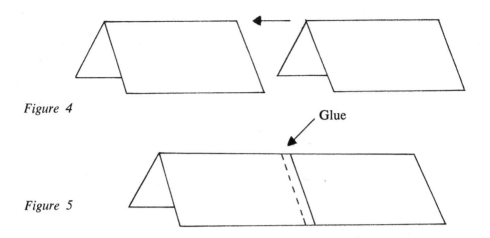

Figure 4

Glue

Figure 5

each 36 inches square. You can choose any pattern that appeals to you.

7. Fold the two sheets in half (Figure 4).

8. Overlap them and glue together as shown in Figure 5.

9. Glue one stick between the folded paper and one on the side of the head (Figure 6). Notice how the tail has been cut.

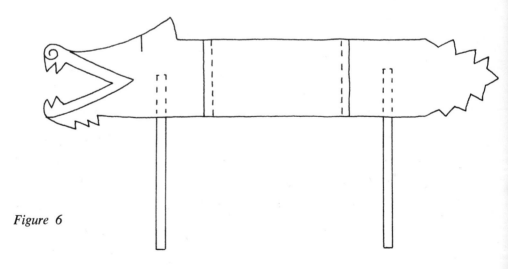

Figure 6

10. Fold the body accordion style, as shown in Figure 7. This will give your dragon a bit of spring.

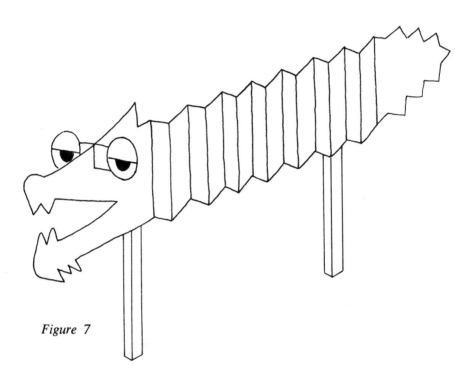

Figure 7

MASKS

In both China and Japan masks have always been used in festival celebrations, as well as in the traditional theater and regional dances and pantomimes. Combined with costume, headdress, or wigs, they enable the audience to instantly recognize the type of character each actor is portraying. The masks are works of art and highly prized by a theatrical troupe.

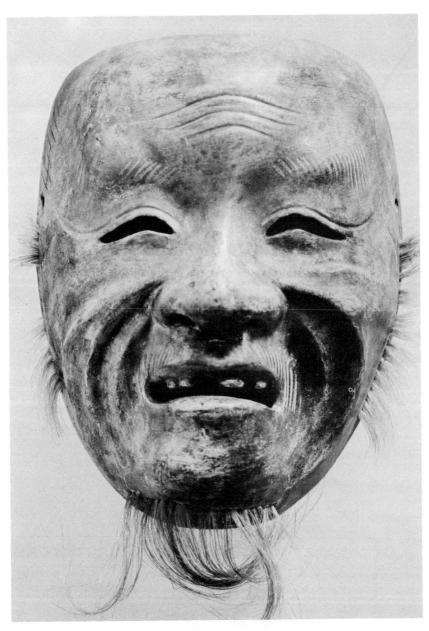

Carved and lacquered wooden mask. Japanese, 17th century. *The Metropolitan Museum of Art, The Howard Mansfield Collection, Gift of Howard Mansfield, 1936*

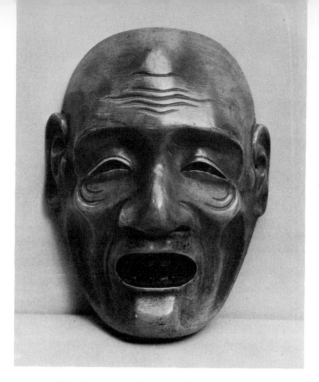

ABOVE: Mask representing an old man, Japanese, 19th century. *The Metropolitan Museum of Art, Fletcher Fund, 1925*

BELOW: Wooden mask of a demon. Japanese, 18th or 19th century. *Courtesy of The Brooklyn Museum*

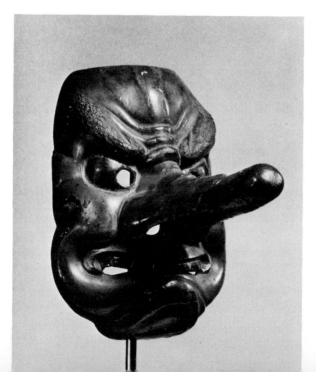

Traditional theater masks represent every type of character conceivable: the young woman, the frightened man, the noble, the warrior, the servant. Their styles range from realistic to grotesque. The richly costumed figures of the actors stand out in contrast to the usually simple and sparse stage sets.

Masks have also assumed importance as objects of art, and are sought after by collectors as household decorations. Miniature masks are also made especially for this purpose.

Miniature Chinese decorative mask, painted metal, 2½ inches high.

We will make our mask to be used as a wall decoration. The two designs shown are inspired by Japanese theater masks.

THEATER MASK

Materials
9 x 12-inch piece of oaktag or lightweight cardboard
9 x 12-inch piece of corrugated cardboard
scissors
X-acto knife (optional)
Elmer's glue

acrylic paints, or colored markers, if desired
paintbrush for use with acrylic paint
pencil
eraser
ruler

How to Make It
1. Sketch the mask shown in Figure 8 on the piece of oaktag. The face should be about 10 inches from top to bottom.
2. Draw the nose separately from the rest of the head (Figure 8). Indicate a slot on the face where the top of the nose will go.

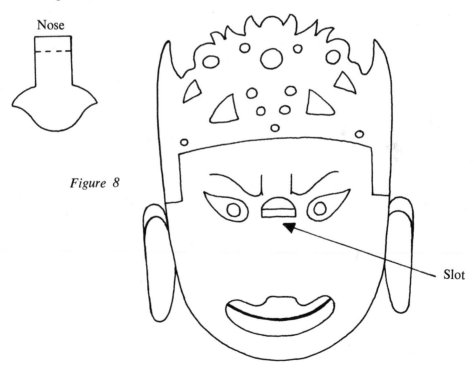

Nose

Figure 8

Slot

49

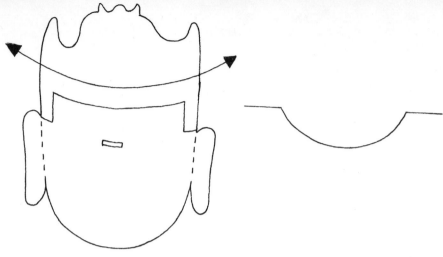

Figure 9

3. Cut out the face and nose with scissors. The slot for the nose can be cut with the X-acto knife, or scissors.

4. Bend the head back as shown in Figure 9, and fold the ears forward as shown. This will give the mask some depth.

5. Insert the nose into the slot and glue it from behind (Figure 10).

6. To decorate the mask, first paint the piece of corrugated cardboard. It will serve as the background. When the paint is dry, glue the ears of the mask onto the background.

Figure 10

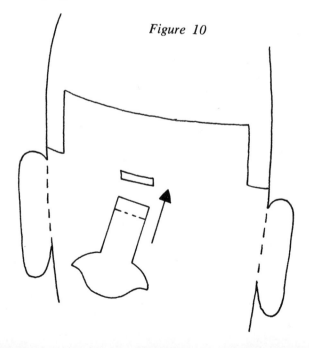

Figure 11

The mask will then keep its curve. Paint the mask or color it with markers.

Figures 11 and 12 show another style of mask, made in the same manner.

Figure 12

Nose

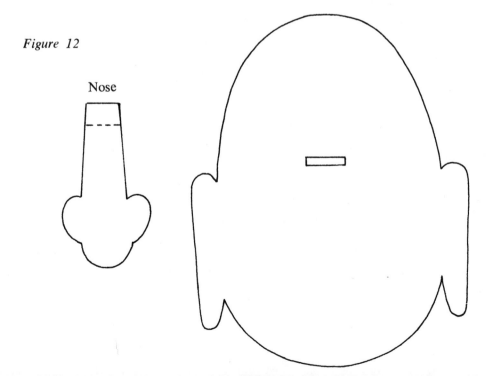

FINGER PUPPETS

Finger puppets possess the drama of the theater masks in miniature. When not being used as puppets, they can serve as decorative accents on a windowsill or bookshelf. Finger puppets are still being made of papier-maché in China today. Ours will also be made of papier-maché.

Materials
1 block plasteline (non-hardening clay)
paper towels
Elmer's glue
paper cup
X-acto knife or single edge razor blade
acrylic paints and brush

How to Make It
1. Model a small form in the shape of a head about 3 x 2 inches. Do not try to include details (Figure 13).

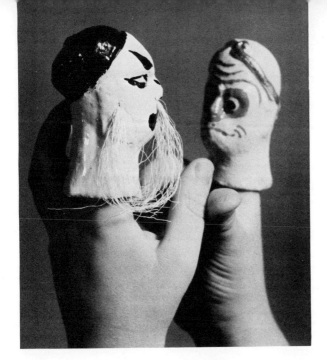

Chinese finger puppets, 3 inches high. *From the collection of the author*

2. Pour some glue into a cup. Tear the paper towels into small pieces about ¾-inch square. Soak the pieces in glue and cover the clay form with them (Figure 14), overlapping the edges.

3. Build up eight layers of paper. Let each layer dry before you apply the next. Make sure that the edges of the paper pieces are smoothed down.

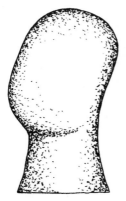

Figure 13

Figure 14

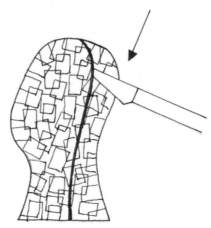

Figure 15

4. When the paper shell is dry and hard, cut the head in half with the X-acto knife or razor blade (Figure 15). Scoop out the clay and glue the shell back together. One additional layer of paper pieces can be glued over the seam.

5. You are now ready to paint your finger puppet. Figures 16 and 17 show two designs. You can derive your own

Figure 16

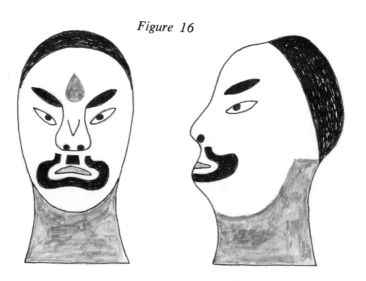

54

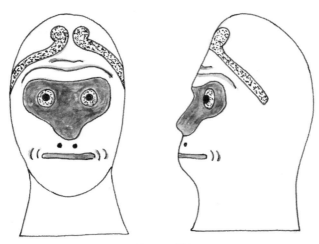

Figure 17

from other designs for masks in this book or combine elements from several different designs. First, decide on a basic color. Dilute the paint with water in a paper cup, and give your puppet three coats of paint. Let each coat dry before applying the next one. Then apply the details to the surface with contrasting colors. If desired, cotton threads can be attached with glue to simulate hair, as in the photograph.

MINIATURE MASKS

Miniature masks about 2 to 3 inches in height can be made in the same way as the finger puppets. Follow the procedure above, but when covering the plasteline form with papier-maché, only cover the front, or "face" of the form. As the mask has no back, you will not have to cut it open to remove the plasteline.

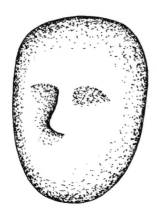

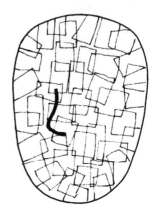

Figure 18   Figure 19

Figure 18 shows a small head form modeled in plasteline. Just suggest the nose and leave out the other features. Figure 19 shows the clay form covered with papier-maché.

Paint the mask in the same way indicated for the finger puppets. You can copy or modify the design of the miniature metal Chinese mask shown, or combine motifs from those shown throughout the book.

Glue a small loop of string to the inside of the mask, at the top. You will then be able to hang it on the wall from a small nail.

Paper-Cutting

Cutting designs from paper has been a popular art for centuries. In the T'ang Dynasty (618–906), decorative cutouts were hung on the doors to celebrate the New Year. The Chinese houses of past times had windows of thin paper, which were treated with oil to make them semi-transparent. Red paper cutout designs were pasted on them to brighten up the rooms year round. The cutouts were also used to decorate presents and various household objects, and as patterns for embroidery and other decorative techniques.

The art of paper-cutting can be simple enough for a

ABOVE: Chinese artist at work creating paper cut designs. *Chinese Information Service, New York*

BELOW AND OPPOSITE: Chinese cut paper designs. *Chinese Cut Paper Designs, Dover Publications, Inc.*

58

young child to enjoy, and can also give an accomplished craftsperson the opportunity to develop designs of great artistry and complexity. Before trying intricate designs in cut paper, first complete the two simple leaf designs below. These will acquaint you with the technical problems of paper-cutting.

LEAF CUTOUTS

Materials

1 package construction paper

1 very fine 4-inch embroidery scissors. In addition, a smaller cuticle scissors would also be helpful.

X-acto knife (optional, but might be of help depending on your design)

pencil and eraser

How to Make It

1. Start with one 9 x 12-inch sheet of construction paper (Figure 1).

2. Sketch the outline of a leaf using the whole sheet of paper, and cut it out with scissors (Figure 2).

Figure 1

Figure 2

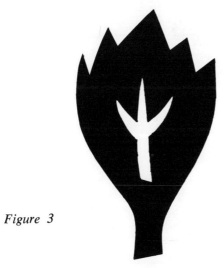

Figure 3

3. Draw the inner leaf structure as shown in Figure 3. Cut it out with scissors or X-acto knife. If you use the X-acto knife, be sure to cut on top of a piece of scrap cardboard to keep the knife sharp. Notice that quite a bit of paper is left around the cutout section.

The next leaf design will require more skill, as more paper will be cut away from the inside of the design.
4. Follow steps 1 and 2 above (Figure 4).

Figure 4

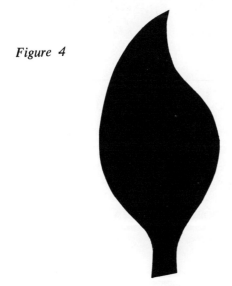

Figure 5

5. Draw inner structure and cut out the sections as shown in Figure 5. Notice how the inner cutouts come closer to the edges. Use the small cuticle scissors or X-acto knife to perform this delicate work.

You are now ready to try your hand at other designs. Look at the examples shown for ideas. You can combine a couple of motifs in one design, if you wish. The designs used for other projects in this book, the masks, for example, can lend themselves easily to this technique.

USES OF CUT PAPER DESIGNS

Your design can be glued on a piece of paper of contrasting color and framed. You need only one or two drops of glue to hold the cutout in place. Then apply drops of glue with a toothpick under thin loose ends of the design.

A cutout design can add a decorative and personal touch to a matted photograph.

Cutouts can also be glued on blocks of wood and coated with matte lacquer. A decorative hook screwed into the top of the block will enable you to hang it on the wall.

Black cut paper design mounted on a wooden board. Note the decorative hanger.

Cut paper design used as a window decoration. The design was glued to the window with a glue for bonding non-porous materials.

You can tape your cut paper design to a windowpane with small pieces of scotch tape, adding a decorative touch to a room just as the Chinese did. For more permanence, you can glue the design, using a glue for bonding non-porous materials.

Stencil-Printing

Both the Chinese and Japanese artists are skilled in the delicate art of stencil-cutting and printing. Designs, hand cut in stiff paper with scissors, knives, and various types of punches, are then used to print on paper or fabric. The designs are inspired by a wide variety of subjects, from dancing people to flowers, birds, and animals.

So fine was the cutting on some of the traditional stencils that the remaining paper had to be reinforced with fine silk thread. The stencil was cut from a strong paper made from mulberry fiber and waterproofed with oil, to keep it from absorbing ink during the printing process. As

Japanese stencil designs. *Japanese Stencil Designs, Dover Publications, Inc.*

Japanese stencil designs. *Japanese Stencil Designs, Dover Publications, Inc.*

a paper stencil cannot last very long, the artist would make enough copies of the same design to serve his purpose. However, for the simple printing projects below, a single stencil of any one design should serve.

Flower motif stenciled onto denim, and circled with decorative studs.

FLOWER STENCIL

Materials

Several 9 x 12-inch sheets of oaktag or thin, non-corrugated cardboard

pencil

eraser

typing paper

scissors

69

Scriber

X-acto knife

X-acto knife
scriber or thin nail
acrylic paint (a tube of any dark color you wish)
¼-inch bristol brush used for oil painting
paper cup for holding paint
You can also use crayons to make your prints, if you wish.

If you intend to use a stencil for many prints, buy a small can of linseed oil. After the stencil has been cut, give it several coats of oil. This will make it somewhat water resistant.

How to Make It
Two basic techniques are used to create a stencil. The first is done by punching small holes along the outline of a design. In the second, areas are cut out with the knife, in somewhat the same technique employed in paper-cutting. Before you attempt a complicated stencil design, try these two techniques on a simple flower motif.

1. Draw a flower design on a piece of cardboard 6 x 6 inches. Then punch holes along the outline with the scriber or nail (Figure 1).

2. Draw the same design again on another square of cardboard, and this time cut out sections with the tip of your X-acto knife (Figure 2). Be sure you do your cutting on a scrap piece of cardboard to keep your knife blade from becoming dull.

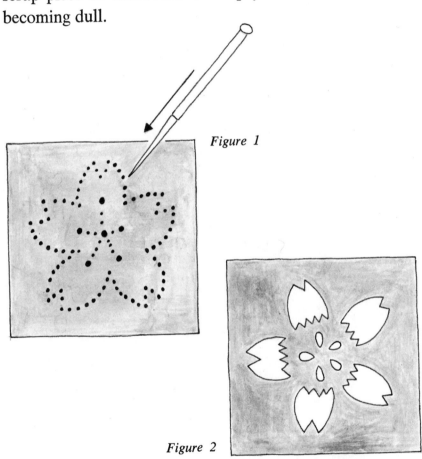

Figure 1

Figure 2

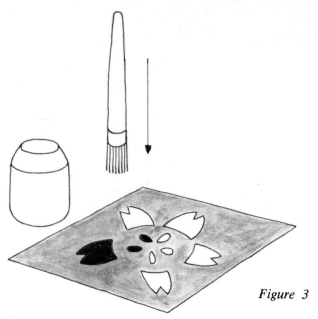

Figure 3

3. You are now ready to print your stencil designs. Squeeze some acrylic paint into a cup. Do not dilute—this is important. If the paint is too thin it will run under the stencil and smear your print. Place the stencil over a sheet of typing paper and dab the paint through the openings (Figure 3). Don't put too much paint on the brush at any one time.

Figure 4 shows the type of print that you will get from the stencil made as shown in Figure 2. Figure 5 shows the type of print that you will get from the stencil shown in Figure 1.

Figure 4

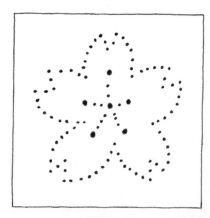

Figure 5

STENCIL DESIGNS

You can adapt the designs shown in this chapter and other chapters in this book. By comparing Figure 6 with Figure 7, you will see how a drawing has to be converted to become a good stencil. There can be no continuous lines, or the stencil will fall apart. Figure 6 shows the original drawing; Figure 7, the finished print.

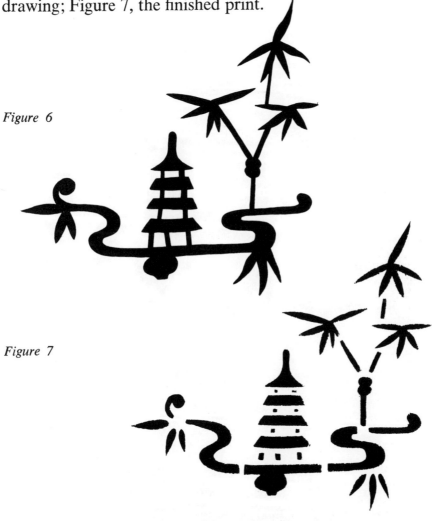

Figure 6

Figure 7

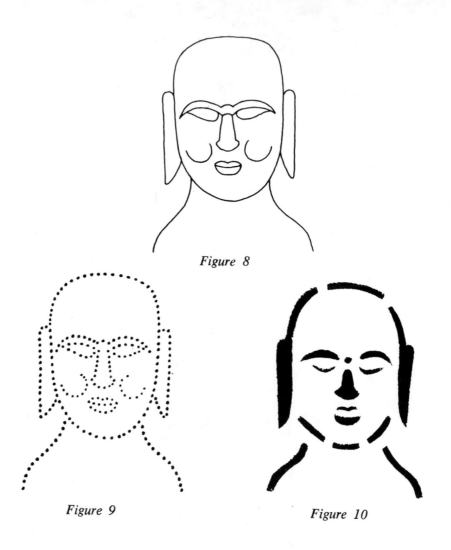

Figure 8

Figure 9

Figure 10

Also compare Figures 8, 9, and 10. Figure 8 is a line drawing sketched from the head of a Chinese sculpture made in the late Ming Dynasty (17th Century). Figure 9 is a print made in dots. Figure 10 is a print made with cutout areas. Notice again how the lines of the design have been broken to give the stencil strength.

74

USES OF STENCIL DESIGNS

Your stencil print can be framed. You can cut your paper to fit the standard size frames available in variety stores.

You can employ the stencil printing technique to make stationery. The Chinese give gifts in beautifully printed envelopes, stenciled with symbolic or pictorial motifs. The design source section at the end of the book, as well as the designs used in many of the other projects, will provide you with a wide choice of motifs to use on your own note-paper and envelopes.

You can also stencil a design on a T-shirt or sweat shirt. Acrylic paint will not come off in the wash, if the washing machine is set for the cold water cycle. Although you can dry the shirt in a drier, the design will probably last longer if you let the shirt air dry on a hanger.

Dragon stenciled on T-shirt.

Crane stenciled on T-shirt.

77

78

Lacquer Ware

The Chinese and Japanese applied their artistry to objects of everyday use. One method was to decorate wooden trays, boxes, and other items in a high gloss lacquer finish. Some items were simply finished with a smooth surface; on others, a design was carved into the lacquer, which had first been built up to a considerable thickness. As many as forty coats of lacquer could be applied to an object. Each coat was allowed to dry and then smoothed with a whetstone before the next one was applied.

Our lacquer tray will be made of cardboard and oaktag in place of wood. Two or three coats of lacquer will be

Carved Chinese lacquer tray. *Photographed at the Chinese Information Service, New York*

enough to achieve the desired look. As we did with the netsuke, instead of attempting intricate carving we will paint a design on the lacquer in a second color.

LACQUER TRAY

Materials
9 x 12-inch piece of corrugated cardboard
1 sheet oaktag
Elmer's glue
scissors
gloss lacquer, sold in small bottles in art supply stores or
    paint stores. You may choose any combination of colors,
    however, red-orange was a popular color used in tradi-

81

Decorative lacquer tray and stand.

tional lacquer ware, so you might choose red-orange for
the background, red for the design, and black for painting the stand.
lacquer-thinner
fine-pointed #2 watercolor brush
ruler
drawing compass
pencil
eraser
scissors

How to Make It
1. Draw a center line on a piece of corrugated cardboard.
Then draw two circles, 4 inches in diameter, centered on
the line (Figure 1). The proportions of the tray will vary,

82

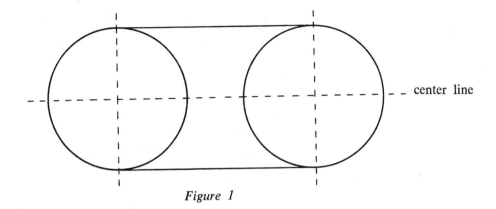

center line

Figure 1

depending upon how far apart you make the circles. Using your ruler, draw two lines connecting the circles as shown in Figure 1. This will be the bottom of your tray.

2. Cut out the resulting shape with scissors.

3. Rule off a ⅜-inch wide strip on the oaktag and cut it out. This will form the sides of the tray.

4. Glue the oaktag strip around the tray (Figure 2). If the strip isn't long enough to go all the way around, you can make another section. You'll find it easier to glue three inches of the strip at a time, letting the glue dry before you continue, than to try to glue the whole strip at once.

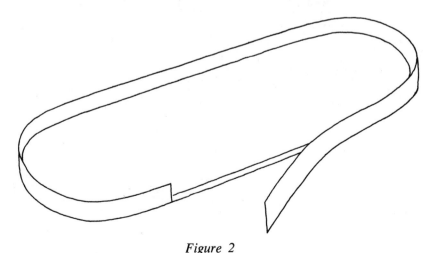

Figure 2

5. Now you are ready to paint your tray. Assuming that you will be using the red-orange and red color scheme, first give the tray two or three coats of red-orange lacquer. Allow each coat to dry before you put on the next.

6. Clean the brush in the thinner.

7. Sketch the design very lightly in pencil on the tray. Figure 3 shows one design, but you can adapt other designs in this book.

8. Paint the design carefully on the surface of the tray in the red lacquer.

Figure 3

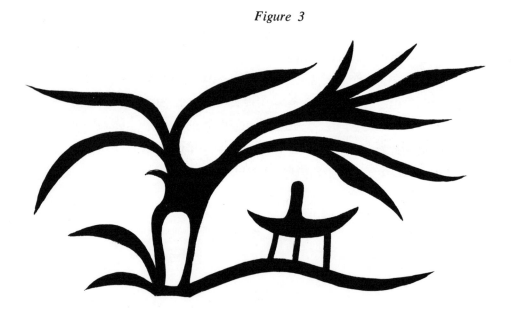

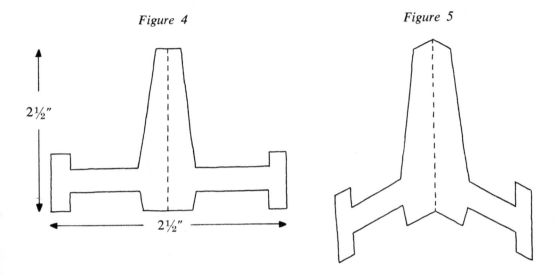

Figure 4

Figure 5

2½"

2½"

Display Stand

9. Figure 4 shows the measurements of the display stand. With ruler and pencil, lay it out on a sheet of oaktag. (Don't use corrugated cardboard, as it wouldn't be suitable for this purpose.)

10. Cut the pattern out with scissors.

11. Fold as shown in Figure 5. To make a straight fold, you can bend the oaktag on the edge of a table. Spread some glue on the inside of the fold so that the stand will hold its angle. Paint the stand with black lacquer.

Although you can vary the proportions of the tray somewhat, keep to the approximate sizes shown. In this way you will stay within the structural strength of the materials used.

LACQUER BOXES

Using the same type of lacquer and brushes used for painting the tray, you can decorate wooden or cardboard boxes. Hobby and craft stores sell a variety of unfinished wood boxes designed for this purpose—wooden cigar boxes can also be used for lacquering. You can obtain small cardboard boxes with covers from jewelry stores or department stores, if you don't already have some around the house.

Lacquer box, Japanese, 16th century. *Courtesy of The Brooklyn Museum*

Decorative lacquer box with *Yang-yin* symbol.

How to Make It

First give the whole box two or three coats of lacquer. If you are using a wooden box, sand between coats with fine sandpaper. Then apply a design in a second color as indicated for the lacquer tray. Figure 6 shows the Chinese *Yang-yin* symbol used on the box photographed. It is a mystical symbol that represents the interaction of opposites in nature, such as the sun and the moon, male and female, light and darkness.

Figure 6

Relief Constructions

Among various types of beautiful carved relief sculptures, Chinese artists made small relief constructions of carved stone or wood. Simple, everyday subjects such as a pot of flowers, birds, or landscape scenes were carved in sections and mounted on a flat background. This background was often painted black to set off the natural color of the carving. Dimensions ranged from approximately five by seven inches to nine by twelve inches, and the finished constructions were often mounted in a deep frame with a glass front.

The plans for the two constructions shown in this chap-

Traditional Chinese relief construction. The carved sections are mounted on the background.

ter will make you familiar with the relief construction technique. You can then create constructions from the other designs shown in this book.

Our constructions will be made from ¼-inch-thick balsa wood, mounted on a cardboard backing. If you have a jigsaw or coping saw you can substitute ¼-inch-thick pine and use ⅛-inch plywood as backing.

89

Crane relief construction with six sections.

CRANE RELIEF

Materials

1 balsa wood strip 36 x 1½ x ¼-inch (36 inches is a standard length, so you will have material left over for another project.)

1 piece of stiff, non-corrugated cardboard, 6 x 9 inches, for
    the backing
emery boards
fine sandpaper
Elmer's glue
X-acto knife
acrylic paint for background, your choice of color
#2 brush for use with acrylic paint
clear lacquer or clear fingernail polish
tracing paper
pencil and eraser
scissors

How to Make It
1. Figure 1 shows a full-scale
drawing of the crane con-
struction.

Figure 1

Figure 2

2. Figure 2 shows the drawing broken down into individual sections. Place a sheet of tracing paper over this page, and trace the sections.

92

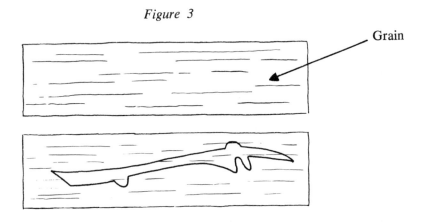

Figure 3

Grain

3. Cut out the paper sections and trace around them lightly in pencil on the balsa wood. Make sure that the longest dimension of each section follows the grain of the wood (Figure 3). This is most important in the slender sections such as the legs, the wings, and the beaks, as it will safeguard against splitting.

4. Cut out the sections with an X-acto knife. Be sure to cut on a scrap of cardboard to keep the knife from dulling.

5. Round off and smooth the edges of the sections with the emery board. Sand the sections with fine sandpaper. Give the finished pieces two coats of clear lacquer or nail polish, sanding lightly between coats.

6. Paint the background cardboard with two coats of acrylic paint. Allow to dry.

7. Glue the sections of the crane on to the background. Don't use too much glue, or it will seep out around the pieces.

Displaying Your Construction

Your relief construction can be framed as you would frame a picture—no glass is needed, however. You can adjust the dimensions of the background so that it will fit a standard ready-made frame. You can choose a large frame or a small frame, depending upon how much background you want to have to set off your construction.

You can also hang your relief without a frame. Glue a loop of cord on the back of the cardboard near the top and hang it from a picture hook.

Boat relief constructions with seven sections. The clouds are painted on the background with acrylic paint.

BOAT RELIEF

Figures 4 and 5 show the drawing and breakdown for a construction of a stylized Chinese boat. Follow the same techniques outlined for the crane.

94

The example shown in the photograph was mounted on a 6 x 8-inch background, but you can make the background any size you wish.

Figure 4

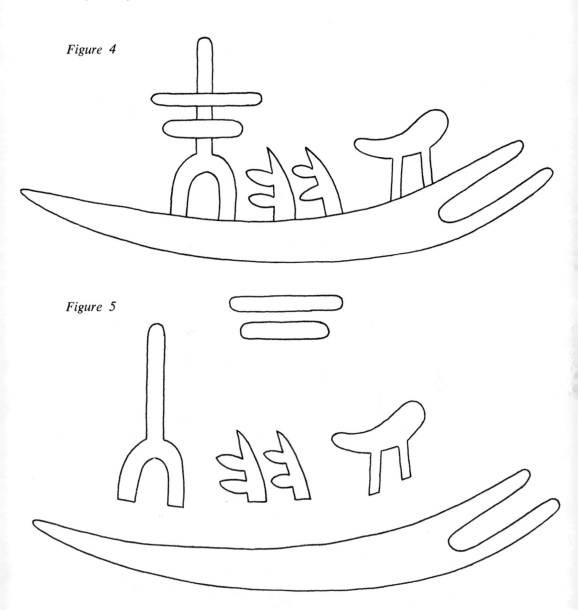

Figure 5

Chinese Rugs

The earliest surviving Chinese rugs were produced in the late Ming Dynasty in the mid-seventeenth century. Some historians feel that rugs were probably being made long before this time.

These rugs were knotted on standing vertical looms, with closely spaced strands of yarn, the warp, strung vertically on the loom frame. The design was knotted by hand around the warp, with about thirty to seventy knots per inch. Some rugs have even been estimated to have as many as one hundred knots per inch!

The yarn used for knotting the design was colored by

Chinese rug, 12th or 13th century. *The Metropolitan Museum of Art, Rogers Fund, 1908*

dyes extracted from flowers, roots, insects, and other natural sources. The subjects depicted in the rugs were similar to those found in other Oriental crafts, such as flowers, animals, and abstract symbols. The Chinese artist approached rug design in many ways, considering the over-all pattern, geometric design, and realistic representation of the subject.

97

Chinese rugs. *Courtesy Macy's, New York*

While we cannot attempt the highly-skilled art of hand-knotting, we will use a popular rug knotting technique called "latchet-hooking." With this technique a design is applied to a mesh canvas, which will serve as our warp. One and a half-inch lengths of rug wool are knotted sixteen knots per inch, using a latchet hook. Although the pile is then much looser than that of Chinese rugs, you will be able to capture some of the quality of Chinese design in your work.

As a rug would be too large a project to describe here, we will make a small hooking that can be used as a pillow cover or wall hanging. Instructions for hooking the Chinese symbol for prosperity will be given; however, you can adapt any design in the book to the method outlined.

Hooked pillow, 18 inches by 18 inches, dark green and yellow on medium green. *Crafted by Roberta Einhorn*

HOOKED PILLOW

Materials

latchet hook

pre-cut rug yarn, in the colors of your choice. The needle-work store can estimate the quantity of yarn needed from your full-scale drawing (see below). Experienced workers prefer 100% wool; however, acrylic yarn is also available and is less expensive.

24 x 24-inch rug canvas

18 x 18-inch sheet of wrapping paper

pencil

eraser

1-inch masking tape

ruler

waterproof marker

How to Use the Latchet Hook

First try to make a few knots with your hook.

1. Push the hook under a strand of mesh (Figure 1). Notice the hook going under strand A. Bend a piece of yarn around the shank of the hook.

2. Hold the handle with your right hand and bend the wool over the latch (Figure 2). (These instructions are for right-handed people, reverse if left-handed.)

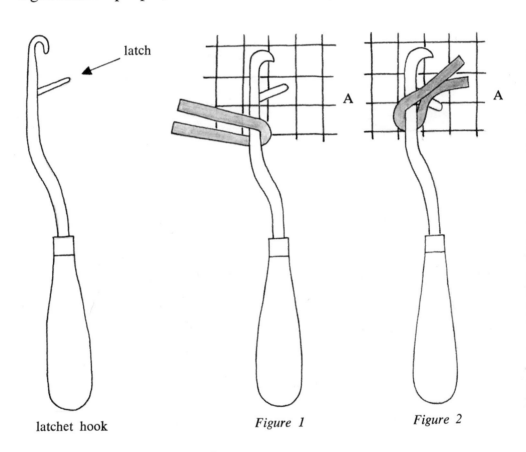

latch

latchet hook

Figure 1

Figure 2

A

A

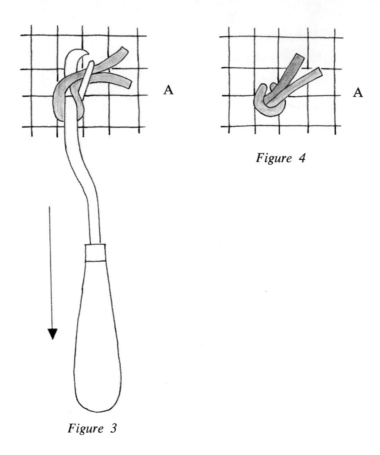

A

A

Figure 4

Figure 3

3. Pull hook down (Figure 3). Notice how the latch closes over the yarn.

4. Keep pulling down. As the hook is pulled, the yarn will be knotted around strand A (Figure 4).

Drawing the Design

1. Draw 4 intersecting lines in pencil as shown in Figure 5, with the center point at the center of the sheet of wrapping paper. Mark off dots 6 inches from the center point as shown.

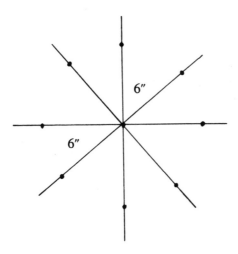

Figure 5

2. Connect the dots to form a circle 12 inches in diameter (Figures 6 and 7). This circle should be centered on the 18 x 18-inch square of paper.

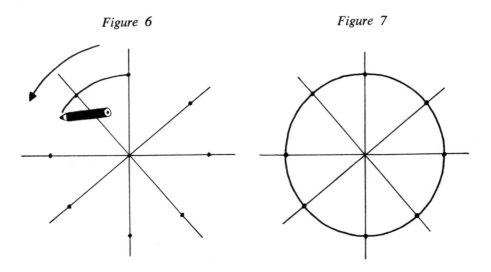

Figure 6   *Figure 7*

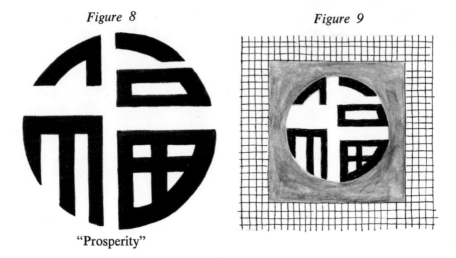

Figure 8　　　　　　*Figure 9*

"Prosperity"

3. With the circle as your starting point, draw the symbol for prosperity shown in Figure 8. Fill in the design with the waterproof marker.

4. Place the paper design under the canvas as shown in Figure 9. You will be able to see the design through the canvas. Go over the design and the outside square on the canvas with your marker. Leave an even border. A waterproof marker is a must. If you clean your hooking it will not run.

Hooking Your Design

1. Tape the edges of the canvas with masking tape to keep them from unraveling.

2. With the latchet hook and the lengths of rug yarn, hook your design in horizontal rows, always working in the same direction. Change yarn colors as you go from one part of the design to the other. You will develop your own personal way of working as you progress.

Mounting Your Work

Your design can be framed as a hanging, or made into a pillow. Unless you are already equipped for pillow-making, it would be easier and less expensive to have a local needlework shop do the job for you—at least, ask their advice. They will be glad to help you.

Now perhaps you can more fully appreciate the patience and artistry that goes into a hand-knotted Chinese rug!

Design Source Material

The following designs can be adapted for the various projects in this book.

OPPOSITE: Flower and leaf motif. ABOVE LEFT: Butterfly motif. ABOVE RIGHT: Flower motif. BELOW: Chinese woman. *Chinese Folk Designs, Dover Publications, Inc.*

Chinese pavilion, 11¼ inches by 11¼ inches. Designed by Donald Pollard.
Engraving designed by Alexander Seidel. Engraved by Roland Erlacher.
Goldwork by Louis Feron. *Courtesy Steuben Glass, New York*

ABOVE: Section of a carved Chinese chest. This motif could easily be adapted to rug-hooking. *Photographed at The Chinese Information Service, New York*

BELOW: Modern Chinese sculptor at work. *Chinese Information Service, New York*

ABOVE: Doll being painted by hand in China. *Chinese Information Service, New York*

BELOW: Modern Chinese pottery worker applying glaze with an air brush. *Chinese Information Service, New York*

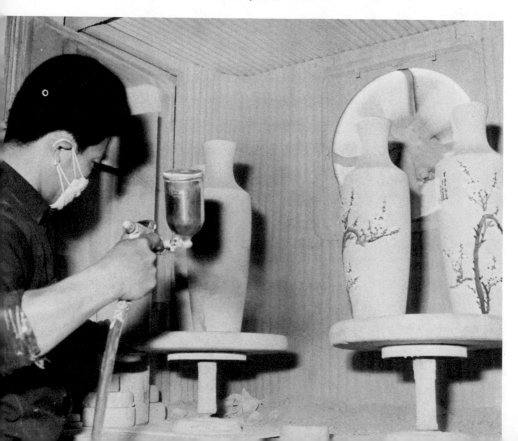

ABOVE: Wood sculptor carving a scene in relief. *Chinese Information Service, New York*

BELOW: Cut-through screen. *Chinese Information Service, New York*

Ceramic figure of a guardian, Chinese, T'ang Dynasty. *Courtesy of The Brooklyn Museum*

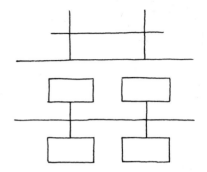

"Double Joy"

"Longevity"

115

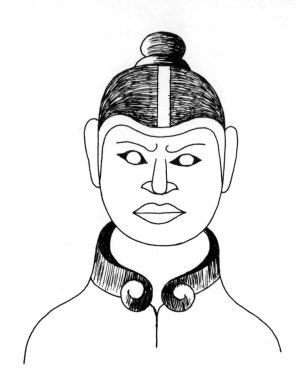

Glossary

Acrylic paint: Plastic base paint that can be diluted with water, but which is waterproof when it dries.

Art: A unique design expressing the maker's feelings and emotions.

Balsa wood: A very lightweight wood which comes from South and Central America. It can be cut with an X-acto knife.

Construction paper: A heavyweight colored paper with a dull finish used in craft work.

Corrugated cardboard: Three-layered paper board with a ridged central layer.

Craft: The use of skill and imagination in the production of things of beauty.

Dilute: To thin out.

Dowel: A round wooden stick.

Emery board: A nail file made of cardboard covered with powdered emery (like sandpaper, but longer lasting).

Grain (of wood): The direction of the wood fibers.

Hooking: To make a rug by drawing pieces of yarn through a coarse mesh and knotting them in place.

Lacquer: A shiny, quick-drying surface coating. Originally, the sap from the native Chinese Lac tree was mixed with colored pigment and used as a paint.

Latchet hook: A long shanked tool with a hooked end and a hinged bar, used in rug hooking.

Oaktag: A thin, lightweight cardboard.

Papier-maché: An art medium made of paper and glue, which can be molded when wet and which hardens when dry.

Pile: A mass of raised loops or tufts covering the surface of a rug or carpet.

Pine wood: A light-colored wood grown in the United States. It is heavier than balsa wood, and requires the use of a saw.

Plasteline: An oily, non-drying, non-hardening clay.

Relief design: A design that is raised from the background.

Rug canvas: A mesh of durable fibers that are cross-hatched to form a series of open squares.

Scriber: A long pointed tool designed for scratching lines in the surface of a hard material.

Slot: A long narrow opening.

Stencil: A cutout used to make prints.

Tracing paper: A thin, semi-transparent paper.

Warp: A series of threads extended lengthwise on a loom used for textile work.

X-acto knife: A razor edge mounted in a handle, used by craftspeople for precise cutting of paper, cardboard, or balsa wood.

Yarn: A continuous strand composed of fibers used in weaving, rug making, and needlework.

Supply Sources

balsa wood, X-acto knives: hobby stores

Elmer's glue, sandpaper, tools: hardware, lumber, and tool supply stores, variety stores

¼-inch pine, plywood: lumberyards

lacquer: paint stores, auto supply stores

tubes of acrylic paint, brushes, oaktag, Elmer's glue: art supply stores

rug-hooking material: needlecraft stores

emery boards, clear nail polish: drug stores

Metric Conversion Chart

1 inch	= 2.54 centimeters or 25.4 millimeters
1 foot	= 0.30 meters
1 yard	= 0.91 meters

1 millimeter	= 0.04 inches
1 centimeter	= 0.39 inches
1 meter	= 39.37 inches, 3.3 feet, or 1.1 yards

The measurements used in this book are inches and feet. To convert to the metric system, round off the numbers as outlined in the following chart.

¼ inch	= 6 mm	4 inches	= 10 cm
⅜ inch	= 9 mm	10 inches	= 25 cm
½ inch	= 1.25 cm	1 foot	= 30 cm
1 inch	= 2.5 cm	2 feet	= 60 cm
2 inches	= 5 cm	3 feet	= 90 cm
3 inches	= 7.5 cm		

Suggestions for
Further Reading

Auboyer, Jeannine, and Goepper, Roger. *The Oriental World*. New York: McGraw-Hill, 1967.

Bradley, Smith, and Weng, Wan-go. *China: A History in Art*. New York: Harper & Row, 1973.

Eaton, Faith. *Dolls in Color*. New York: Macmillan, 1975.

Hawley, W. H. *Chinese Folk Designs*. New York: Dover Publications, Inc., 1949.

Hay, John. *Masterpieces of Chinese Art*. New York Graphics Society, 1974.

Liebetrau, Preben. *Oriental Rugs in Color*. New York: Macmillan, 1962.

Menten, Theodore. *Chinese Cut-Paper Designs*. New York: Dover Publications, Inc., 1975.

Neave, W. B. R. *Chinese Ceramics*. New York: St. Martin's Press, 1975.

Ryerson, Egerton. *The Netsuke of Japan*. Cranbury, New Jersey: A. S. Barnes & Co., 1958.

Scobey, Joan. *Rugs and Wall Hangings*. New York: Dial Press, 1974.

Stern, Harold P. *Birds, Beasts, Blossoms and Bugs: The Nature of Japan*. New York: Harry N. Abrams, 1976.

Sullivan, Michael. *The Arts of China*. Berkeley: University of California Press, 1973.

Tuer, Andrew W. *Japanese Stencil Designs*. New York: Dover Publications, Inc., 1967.

Index

* indicates photograph

125

126